THE
CLOWN THAT
LOST HIS
FUNNY

Lauren Lukaszewski

by Lauren K. Lukaszewski
illustrated by Joyeeta

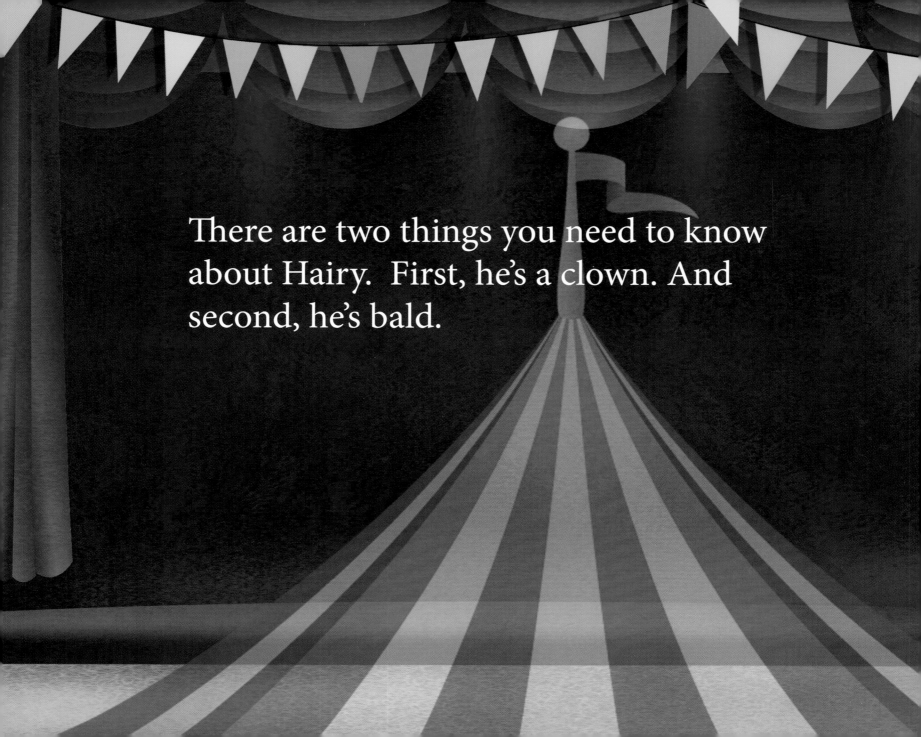

There are two things you need to know about Hairy. First, he's a clown. And second, he's bald.

Hairy's twin brother is a banker.

Hairy didn't want to be a boring banker.

So when he was old enough, he got a job at the circus.

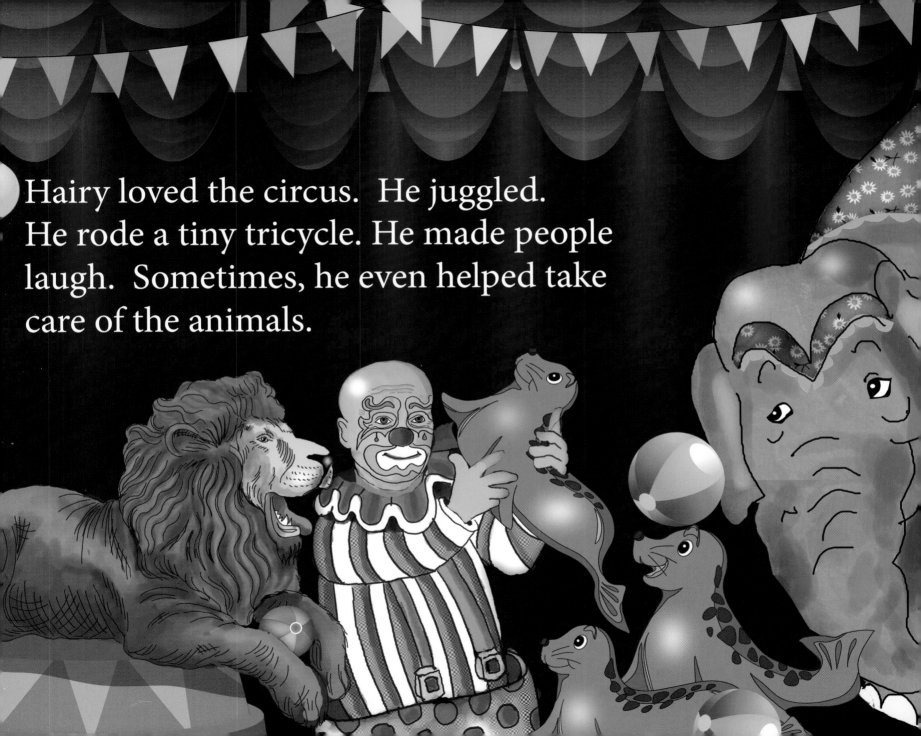

Hairy loved the circus. He juggled.
He rode a tiny tricycle. He made people
laugh. Sometimes, he even helped take
care of the animals.

One day at the circus, Hairy was juggling three bowling pins. He didn't notice the elephant inching closer and closer to him.

It turns out, Hairy had some peanuts in his pocket.

And as you know, elephants love peanuts.

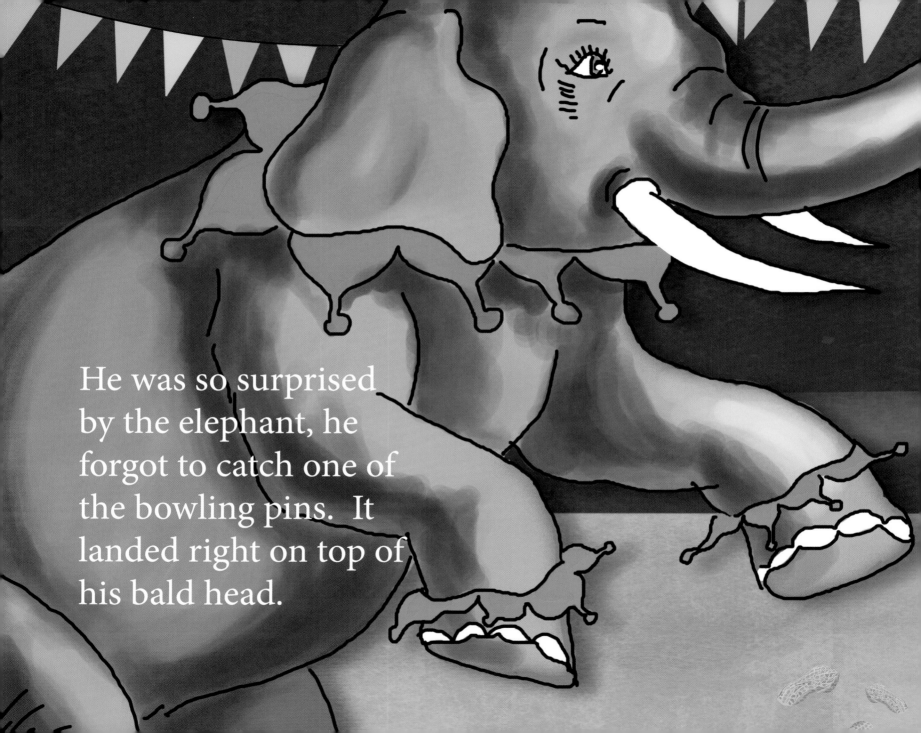

He was so surprised by the elephant, he forgot to catch one of the bowling pins. It landed right on top of his bald head.

The next thing Hairy remembered was waking up in the hospital.

When the nurses came to check on him, Hairy tried to tell them jokes. But none of his jokes were funny.

In the hospital, a sad thing happened... Hairy lost his funny.

Now a clown that isn't funny can't work at the circus. Hairy had to find a new job.

His brother the banker offered him a job at the bank. And since Hairy didn't have any other options, he said yes.

Hairy didn't like working at the bank.

He had to count money.

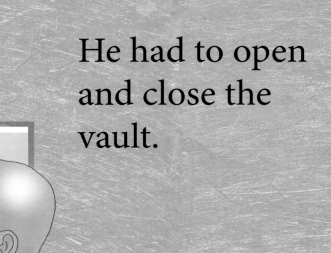

He had to open
and close the
vault.

There was
absolutely
nothing funny
about his job.

One day, a little boy came into the bank. The boy looked very sad.

"Why are you sad?" asked Hairy.

"Because we have to move to a different state and I'm going to miss all my friends. My mom said I should get all the money out of my bank account," said the boy.

"Hmmm...I'm not sure your money is in your bank account."

"WHAT?" said the sad boy.

"I think it's......right here!" said Hairy.

At that moment, Hairy reached behind the boy's left ear and pulled out a golden coin.

The boy smiled the biggest smile Hairy had ever seen.

"Why you're the funniest banker
I ever met," said the boy.

Then Hairy realized he never *really* lost his funny....

He had it all along.

DISCUSSION QUESTIONS FOR PARENTS

One of the big lessons in this book is to stay true to yourself. Hairy's situation and environment changed, but who he truly was stayed the same. Sometimes, it takes lots of conversations and experiences to help us understand who we really are. Here are some questions you can ask your child to get a conversation going.

1. Ever since Hairy was a kid, he wanted to be a clown. What do you want to be when you grow up?
2. Hairy found himself doing a job he didn't like. Have you ever had to do jobs you didn't like?
3. Have you ever lost anything only to realize you never really lost it?

DISCUSSION AND ACTIVITIES FOR TEACHERS

1. Have you ever been to the circus? What do you think would be the most fun job there?
2. Do you think Hairy actually got his job back at the circus?
3. Onomatopeia is the use of words that imitate sounds. Forshadowing are hints to prepare a reader for what is to come. Irony is used to suggest the opposite of a usual meaning. Can you find these literary techniques in the book?

For more about Hairy, visit hairytheclown.com.

KICKSTARTER

Thanks to everyone who backed this project on KickStarter: Andy McQuaid, Tony McCollum, Sharon Green, Amy Bloye, Trevor Walsh, Sunshine Black, Rodney and Sarah Anderson, Paul Pittman, Dave Anderson, Jeff Henderson, Shawn Wood, Scott Winter, Bryan and Karen Isbell, The Wilmingtons, Michael and Josh, Bob Franquiz, Scott Slayton, Rich Birch, Will Goodwin, Mark Clement, Kristy McCarthy, Jake Dudley, Collin Wood, Elizabeth Carswell, Jordi Fita, David Walters, David Brower, Lami, Tamara Siuda, Tally Wilgis, Andrea Dreyfus, Tadd Grandstaff, Jeff Kapusta, Casey Graham, Carol Jones, Brad Dutton, Dan Stauffer, Sheri Davis, Jody May, Rob Whitmire, Courtney Templeton, Paul Cool, Melissa Wilkins, Jeremiah Martin, Becca Harper, Kate Fleming, Larry Boatright, Kaela Bostic, Debbie Dickey, Michelle Valigursky, Ken Friar, Charlie Pharis, Brent Guice, Robert Booth, Lindsy Thorpe, Van Baird, Alan Vukas, David Johnson, Jim Akins, Marcia Campbell, Rebecca Machacek, Brian Dodd, Michelle Vetter, Laurel Beard, Ian McMahon, Jason Burns, Johnny Hunt, Charles Boehmig, Terry Lowry, Nic Burleson, Jacquine Newell, Kristen Franklin, Penny Davis, Bobby Williams, Jonathon Bone, Dan DeReuter, Alli Enderle, Ryan Boon, The Tyszs, Tiffani Ainsworth, Tim O'Peters, Jenn Skinner, Annette Morrison, Kristy Smith, Allie Towsend, Stacy Wood, Justin Davis, Sean Krumhauer, Charles Land, Kristie Anderson, Aaron Skinner,
Michael Lukaszewski, Sr., Chris Goeppner, Mitch Moyer, Joyce Kreider, Thomas Bachmayer, Andrew Forman, Walter Brigman, Shane Hart, Soundsgood Ministries, Bryan Davidson, The Lawrences, Carissa Figgins and RKRS.

For all the people who believed in me,
and my dad who helped make this
book a reality.

About the Author: Lauren was born in Jacksonville, Florida and lives with her family near Atlanta, Georgia. She wrote this book when she was a fifth grader at Alpharetta Elementary School. Lauren likes reading, writing, swimming, sushi, and history. Read Lauren's blog at laurenlukaszewski.com.

About the Illustrator: Joyeeta lives in Pune, India with her husband and seven year old daughter. She started her career in fashion design, and now fuels her creative passion through illustrating children's books. Learn more at joyee14.wix.com/artsutrajoyee